KIDS
COOKBOOK

BRIDGET JONES

A QUANTUM BOOK

This book is produced by
Quantum Publishing Ltd.
6 Blundell Street
London N7 9BH

ISBN 1-86160-910-8

QUMCFK-R

Printed in Singapore by
Star Standard Industries Pte Ltd

Contents

BEFORE YOU START

Cooking is fun. To make sure you enjoy cooking and the food tastes good enough to eat, read through these notes first.

★ Always ask if you can cook.
★ Make sure you have an adult in the kitchen to help.
★ Put an apron on to keep your clothes clean. Having an apron on also keeps your clothes away from the food and the cooker.
★ Keep long sleeves rolled up out of the way.
★ Wash your hands really well in hot soapy water.
★ Read through the recipe first.
★ Find all the ingredients and put them out ready.
★ Set out all the utensils.
★ Keep a clean, damp dish cloth near to wipe up any mess.

Now you may begin!

SAFE AND CLEAN

Remember that what you are cooking is going to be eaten. The food must be kept clean all the time. If you have an accident while you are cooking, there will not be any food to eat. So always remember the S + C Rules.

★ Make sure you have an adult near when you are using the hob, grill or cooker.
★ Always use oven gloves when you are handling hot dishes.
★ Put a heatproof mat on the work surface before taking hot pans and dishes from the hob, grill or oven.
★ When you put pans on the hob make sure the handles are pointing to the side, not out in front where you may knock them.
★ Always watch food which is cooking under the grill.

★ As soon as you have finished cooking food turn off the heat.
★ Take extra care when using knives. Make sure the knife is the right size so that you can hold it properly.
★ Keep your fingers out of the way when cutting and chopping. Cut slowly to get it right.
★ Always wash your knife and scrub the board after cutting raw fish, meat or chicken and before cutting up any other ingredients.
★ Keep the work surface clean by wiping up as you are cooking.
★ If you spill anything wipe it up at once.
★ Don't forget to wash up and tidy the kitchen!

USING THE MICROWAVE

The microwave cooker is safe to use because it is not as hot as the hob or oven. You must remember to use it properly.

★ Never put baking tins, cooking foil or wire bag ties in the microwave.
★ Never switch the microwave on without any food in it.
★ Take care when setting the timer. Check you have the right cooking time.
★ Check that you are using the correct power setting.
★ Always cook food for a short time. Take it out and stir or turn the food before cooking again for a short time.
★ Remember that the food gets very hot. Use an oven glove to take dishes from the microwave.
★ When you think the food is cooked, check that it is cooked through. Stir wet foods before serving. If parts of the food are cold or not cooked, then put it back in the microwave and cook for another short time.

★ There are microwave notes for some of the recipes. The times are for a 650 watt cooker. Ask what power your microwave cooks at and check that it is the same. If it has a lower power, the cooking will take a little longer. If it has a higher power the food will cook more quickly.

WEIGHING AND MEASURING INGREDIENTS

All the recipes in this book give the quantities in metric and Imperial measures. You must follow one set of quantities for each recipe.

WEIGHING

You need a pair of kitchen scales to weigh food. Practise by weighing some vegetables. When you have tried weighing a few items you will see how your scales work.

MEASURING TEASPOONS AND TABLESPOONS

When a recipe tells you to add 1 teaspoon of something, or 2 tablespoons, you must use proper measuring spoons.

★ Measuring spoons come in small sets. They include ¼ teaspoon, ½ teaspoon, 1 teaspoon and 1 tablespoon. Each spoon will have the size written on it.
★ Use the right size spoon. Fill the spoon with the ingredient. Use a knife to level the top of the spoon when measuring dry ingredients.
★ Hold the spoon steady and level for a few seconds when measuring liquid to check that it is full.

MEASURING LIQUID

★ Pour the liquid into a measuring jug and put it on a level surface.
★ Look at the side of the jug to see if the liquid is up to the mark you want. If

not add more. If there is too much in the jug, pour a little out, put it back on the level and check again.

WHAT IS A . . .

KITCHEN KNIFE

For chopping up food you will need a sharp kitchen knife, also called a chef's knife. Make sure it is not too big to handle.

PALETTE KNIFE OR BLUNT KNIFE

This is a knife with a rounded end. It does not have a sharp edge. Some dinner knives are blunt so they may be used instead of a palette knife. A palette knife is used to lift biscuits off baking trays or to spread butter, icing or soft cheese.

CHOPPING BOARD

When you cut something always use a chopping board. Make sure that the board is safe and firm on the work surface. If the surface is slippery, put a piece of absorbent kitchen paper under the board. Plastic boards are more advisable than wooden ones because they are easier to clean. When you have finished cooking you must scrub the chopping board with a brush and kitchen cleaner.

GRATER

There are lots of different types. They have fine or coarse blades. Always take care when grating food – it is easy to grate the end of your fingers and it hurts!

LEMON SQUEEZER

Some recipes tell you to squeeze the juice from a lemon or orange. You have to cut the fruit in half, then hold one half on a lemon squeezer. Twist the fruit around, pressing it down on the squeezer to get all the juice out.

WHISK

This is used for whisking eggs and for whipping cream. A hand whisk is made up of wire loops and a handle. A rotary whisk has 2 metal whisks that are turned by you turning a handle. An electric whisk is very quick but you should never use one unless you have an adult with you.

SIEVE

This is used for sifting flour that may be lumpy. It is also used for making a purée, or paste, out of food. Stand the sieve firmly over a bowl before putting the food in it.

PASTRY BRUSH

This is a small brush made for kitchen use. A pastry brush is used for brushing pastry and other foods with egg, milk or water. After you have grated fruit rind, use a pastry brush to brush all the rind off the grater.

COLANDER

A bowl with holes in it. This is used to drain food. Cooked pasta is drained in a colander. Shredded cabbage or lettuce may be put in a colander to drain when it has been washed. Always put the colander in the sink or over a bowl.

BAKING TRAY

A flat metal tray used for baking biscuits and other foods in the oven. Sometimes a baking tray is covered with paper or cling film and used to put delicate foods on while they are chilling or setting.

WIRE RACK

This is used to cool hot food and may be round, square or oblong. Some cakes and biscuits become soggy underneath if they are not put on a wire rack to cool.

PIPING BAG

A tough bag made of plastic or material. The bag has a pointed end with a small hole in it. You put a nozzle in the hole, then fill the bag with cream or other food. When you fold the ends of the bag together and squeeze, the food comes out in patterns.

NOZZLE

There are lots of different nozzles. Tiny nozzles are used to decorate cakes. Very big nozzles are used to pipe mashed potato into swirls. Medium sized nozzles are used for piping whipped cream on cakes.

HOW TO . . .
CHOP AN ONION

Chop the ends off the onion.

Peel the onion.

Cut into thin slices.

Chop the slices into small pieces.

HEATPROOF MAT

Before you take a hot pan or cooking container off the hob or from the oven, place a heatproof mat on the work surface. Put the hot pan on the mat so the work surface doesn't get scorched.

CLEAN MUSHROOMS

1 Cut off the ends of the mushroom stalks.
2 Mushrooms must not be put into a bowl of water. Rinse them 1 at a time under cold running water. Hold the mushroom like an umbrella under the water, with the stalk down and the rounded side up.
3 Rub any dirt off the rounded side with your fingers. Shake the water off the mushroom. Put the mushroom with the stalk up on double thick absorbent kitchen paper. Pat it dry.

MAKE BREADCRUMBS

1 Cut the crusts off a piece of bread.
2 Rub the bread on the coarse side of a grater, letting the crumbs fall into a bowl.
3 If you have a blender or food processor, then ask an adult if they will make some breadcrumbs for you in that.

RUB FAT INTO FLOUR

1 Use a knife to cut the fat into small pieces.
2 Wash and dry your hands in cold water. If your hands are warm the fat will become very sticky.
3 Use just the tips of your fingers to pick up a lump of fat and some flour. Lift it slightly above the mixture.
4 Rub the fat and flour together between your thumb and fingertips. Let the mixture fall back into the bowl.
5 The mixture is ready when there are not any large lumps of fat. It should look like fresh breadcrumbs.

SEPARATE AN EGG

Tap the egg in the middle to break the shell. Pull the shell lightly apart with your thumbs.

Let the white run into the basin and keep the yolk in the shell.

Open the shell into two pieces. Keep the yolk in one half.

Pour the white from each half into the basin. Tip the yolk into a second basin.

FILL A PIPING BAG

1 Put the nozzle in the piping bag.
2 Put the nozzle end of the bag in a measuring jug and fold the rest of the bag down around the outside of the jug.
3 Use a spoon to put the cream or other mixture in the bag.
4 Gather up the ends of the bag and twist them together.

PIPE CREAM

Put the nozzle in the piping bag.

Put the nozzle end in a measuring jug. Fold the bag around the jug.

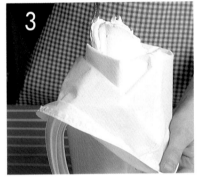

Put the cream in the bag using a spoon.

Hold the nozzle just above what you want to pipe and squeeze the bag to push out the cream.

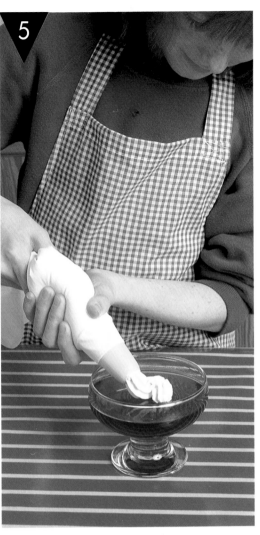

Move the bag around to make a swirl.

A NOTE TO ADULTS

The recipes in this book include some that are very simple and others that are more suitable for older children. Always supervise young children when they are cooking. Encourage your children to cook but always make sure they ask to use the kitchen so you know what they are doing. If they are preparing food that involves using the hob, oven or grill, then stay with them. No matter what age, always check what they are doing, which foods they are using, the utensils and the results.

COOKING FOR FUN

▶· Crazy Crackers ·◀

Make these using other ingredients – try using pieces of cooked ham or salami, small pieces of red or green pepper, cut up small pickled gherkins or use sliced celery sticks. Have fun making lots of different patterns or try these ideas.

1 To make the boats, spread the cream cheese on 4 crackers and make small peaks in it to look like waves. Cut 8 small triangles out of the cheese slice to look like sails. Cut the tomato slices in half.

2 Put a piece of tomato on each cracker to look like the bottom of the boat and put the cheese triangles above the tomatoes to look like sails. Leave a little space all around the sails. Put strips of cucumber between the sails to make masts and add a small triangle of cucumber peel to look like a flag.

3 For the faces, mix the ketchup with the cream cheese and spread it on 4 crackers. Break the potato sticks and put them on the crackers to look like hair. Add 2 raisins to each to look like eyes. Cut the radishes into quarters. Put 1 piece of radish in the middle of the face to look like a nose, making sure the red skin is facing up. Turn the other wedges of radish on their sides and place on the crackers to look like mouths.

4 To make the flowers, mix the cream cheese with the parsley and spread it on 4 crackers. Use a small flower shaped biscuit cutter or small round cutter to cut 4 pieces out of the cheese. Put 1 on each cracker.

5 Cut a thin strip from the middle of each cucumber slice and put these on the crackers to look like the stem of the flower. Put the other pieces of cucumber at the bottom of the stems to look like leaves. If the cucumber is too big, cut the pieces in half.

6 Put a little tomato ketchup on a saucer. Dip a cocktail stick in the ketchup and dot it in the middle of the cheese flowers. Put lots of small dots of ketchup in each flower.

12 large square cream crackers or water biscuits

Boats
2 tablespoons cream cheese
1 cheese slice
2 slices tomato
4 small sticks cucumber
4 tiny triangles cucumber peel

Faces
½ teaspoon tomato ketchup
2 tablespoons cream cheese
a few potato sticks
8 raisins
2 radishes

Flowers
2 tablespoons cream cheese
1 tablespoon chopped parsley
1 cheese slice
a little tomato ketchup
4 slices cucumber

Makes 12

▶· Cheese Savouries ·◀

3 cream crackers or water biscuits
100 g/4 oz curd cheese
2 teaspoons tomato ketchup
2 small bags salted crisps
(pick your favourite flavour)
a few parsley sprigs

Makes 15

1 Put the biscuits or crackers in a polythene bag and lay it flat on the work surface. Fold the end of the bag under. Use a rolling pin to crush the biscuits. Do this gently, until the biscuits are all in crumbs.

2 Put the curd cheese in a basin. Use a plastic or wooden spoon to stir the cheese. Add the biscuit crumbs and stir well until the cheese and crumbs are mixed.

3 Add the ketchup and stir until it is evenly mixed with the cheese.

4 Use your fingers to crush the crisps in their packets. Do this gently so as not to burst the bags. When all the crisps are broken into little pieces, turn them out on to a large plate.

5 Wash and dry your hands. Take a teaspoonful of the cheese mixture and roll it into a ball. Do this quickly and put the ball on the crushed crisps. Roll the cheese ball in the crisps until it is covered all over.

6 Shape all the mixture into balls and place them on a plate. You may put the balls into plain paper sweet cases if you like. Gently press a tiny sprig of parsley on top of each ball.

◄·Clever Cookies·◄

24 plain sweet biscuits
jam or chocolate spread
175 g/6 oz icing sugar
1–2 tablespoons water

Decoration
coloured sugar strands
chocolate buttons
a few glacé cherries
mimosa balls
angelica

Makes 12

1 Spread 12 biscuits with jam or chocolate spread and press the other biscuits on top.

2 Sift the icing sugar into a basin. Add 1 tablespoon of the water and mix it with the sugar, adding some or all of the remaining water to make a smooth icing. The icing must not be too runny.

3 Use a teaspoon to put some icing in the middle of each Clever Cookie, spreading it out a little to cover the top. Set about 4 of the cookies aside to dry, then sprinkle them with sugar strands.

4 Press a ring of chocolate buttons on to 4 of the cookies while the icing is wet. Overlap the buttons neatly. Cut 2 glacé cherries in half and put half in the middle of the ring of buttons.

5 Put jellied sweets or cake decorations on the other cookies.

6 Leave the icing to set before putting the cookies on a plate.

▸·banana date logs·◂

1 small banana
1 tablespoon icing sugar
100 g/4 oz chopped cooking dates
4 tablespoons desiccated coconut
50 g/2 oz plain sweet biscuits
4 tablespoons drinking chocolate

Makes 16

1 Peel the banana and break it into pieces. Put the pieces in a basin and use a fork to mash them. Sift in the icing sugar and mix in the dates and the desiccated coconut.

2 Put the biscuits in a polythene bag and fold the end over. Use a rolling pin to crush them into fine crumbs. Stir the crushed biscuits into the mixture.

3 Wash and dry your hands. Take small spoonfuls of the mixture and roll them into 16 balls. Flatten the balls and shape them into logs about 2.5 cm/1 in long.

4 Sprinkle the drinking chocolate on a plate. Roll the logs in the drinking chocolate to coat them completely. Put them into paper sweet cases and put them in the refrigerator for at least 30 minutes.

jammy birthday cake

1 bought plain cake (any type will do)
175 g / 6 oz jam (your favourite flavour)
75 g / 3 oz desiccated coconut
50 g / 2 oz multi-coloured glacé cherries
angelica
birthday candles and holders
piece of red ribbon

Makes about 10 slices

1 Place the cake on a flat plate. Use a spoon to put the jam on the top of the cake, near the middle. Scrape all the jam off the spoon with a knife.

2 Spread the jam evenly over the top of the cake, taking care that it does not fall down the side. Sprinkle the coconut all over the jam in a nice thick layer.

3 Use a small knife to cut the cherries into quarters. Cut small, thin strips of angelica.

4 Make cherry flowers on the top of the cake. Put pieces of cherry together so they look like petals and use a piece of angelica for a stalk.

5 Stick birthday candles in their holders between the cherry flowers. Use a pastry brush to brush any crumbs and bits of coconut off the plate. Tie a bow of ribbon around the side of the cake.

►·chocolate orange fingers·◄

1 bought loaf cake (plain or chocolate)
4 tablespoons chocolate spread
1 tablespoon orange marmalade
white chocolate buttons
jellied orange slices

Makes 10

1 Cut the cake into 5 thick slices. Cut each slice in half through the middle to make 10 long fingers. Put the fingers on a board with the crust side of the cake upwards.

2 Put the chocolate spread in a basin and gradually beat in the marmalade, adding a spoonful at a time. Spread some of this topping over the cake fingers, making small peaks or swirls in it.

3 Press a line of white chocolate buttons on top of some of the fingers. Put some jellied orange slices on top of the other fingers. Arrange the fingers on a plate to serve.

It's Simple to Start Cooking

▸·nutty eggs ·◂

4 eggs
100 g/4 oz cottage cheese
2 tablespoons crunchy peanut butter
salt and pepper
4 slices cucumber

Makes 8

1 Put the eggs in a small saucepan and pour in enough cold water to cover them. Put the saucepan on the hob and turn the heat to high. When the water boils, turn the heat to medium. Boil the eggs for 10 minutes.

2 While the eggs are boiling, put the cottage cheese in a basin and mash it with a fork until all the lumps are broken. The cheese should be fairly smooth.

3 Turn off the heat. Take care when lifting the saucepan off the hob. Put it in the sink and pour off the boiling water. Run cold water on to the eggs and leave them until they are cold.

4 Tap the cold eggs on the work surface to crack their shells, then pull off all the shells. This is easy if you break the very fine skin that lies just underneath the shell. Put the shelled eggs on a plate.

5 Cut the eggs in half lengthways. Use a teaspoon to scoop out the yolks. Add the yolks to the cottage cheese and mash them with it. Add the peanut butter and mash the mixture together. Stir in a little salt and pepper.

6 Use a teaspoon to put the cottage cheese mixture into the egg whites. Place the stuffed eggs on a plate. Cut the cucumber slices into quarters and stick 2 pieces into the stuffing on each egg.

⊪▶·red hot jackets·◀⊩

2 large potatoes
a little cooking oil
butter

Serves 4

1

2

3

MICROWAVE TIP
Potatoes cook quickly in the microwave.
Put them on a double-thick piece of
absorbent kitchen paper. Prick them in a
few places with a fork. Cook them on Full
Power for 12–15 minutes, rotating their
positions halfway through cooking.

Set the oven at 200°C/400°F/gas 6. Wash the potatoes, scrubbing them with a small brush. Cut out any bad bits, then dry the potatoes on absorbent kitchen paper. Prick them in a few places and put on a baking tray.

Brush a little oil all over the potatoes, then bake them for 1–1¼ hours. Use oven gloves to remove the baking tray from the oven. Hold 1 potato with a clean tea-towel and carefully stick a fork into it. If the potato feels soft in the middle it is cooked. If the middle of the potato still feels hard, then it should be cooked for another 5 minutes before testing it again. Turn the heat off.

Hold one side of the potato with a tea-towel and cut it in half. Place on individual plates, then top each half with a knob of butter. Cut the other potato in the same way. If you like try some of the following tremendous toppings and fillings.

potatoes with creamy ham topping

2 baked potatoes
100 g/4 oz soft cheese
100 g/4 oz cooked ham
salt and pepper
8 slices cucumber

1   Bake the potatoes and cut them in half following the recipe for Red Hot Jackets. Turn the oven off.

2   Put the soft cheese in a basin. Cut the ham into slices, then cut across the slices to small dice. Mix the ham with the soft cheese. Mix in a little salt and pepper.

3   Use a teaspoon to pile the cheese and ham on top of the potatoes. Stick 2 cucumber slices into the topping on each potato and serve at once.

beany potatoes

1   Bake the potatoes and cut them in half following the recipe for Red Hot Jackets. About 5 minutes before the end of the cooking time for the potatoes, turn the baked beans into a small saucepan and put them on the hob. Turn the heat to medium. When the beans are bubbling, turn the heat down to the lowest setting.

2 baked potatoes
225 g/8 oz can baked beans
25 g/1 oz cheese (optional)

2   Grate the cheese if you are using it. Turn the oven and hob off. Use oven gloves to take the potatoes from the oven and put them on plates. Top each potato with some of the beans. Sprinkle each one with a little grated cheese if you like.

OTHER SIMPLE TOPPINGS FOR BAKED POTATOES

★   A spoonful of crunchy peanut butter
★   A spoonful of cottage cheese sprinkled with chopped parsley
★   A spoonful of mayonnaise mixed with a little tomato ketchup
★   A frankfurter with 6 slices of cucumber and a little mustard
★   Two slices of salami and a sliced tomato
★   A spoonful of flaked tuna fish topped with thick natural yogurt

▪►· bean feast ·◄▪

2 large round crusty bread rolls
½ small onion
2 tablespoons vegetable oil
¼ teaspoon dried sage
225 g/8 oz can baked beans
50 g/2 oz cheese

Serves 2

1 Use a sharp knife to cut a small cap off the tops of the rolls. Take care not to cut your fingers. Save the slices. Pull the soft middle out of the rolls, leaving just the crisp shells. Be careful not to break the crusts.

2 Put the soft bread on a board and cut it into small pieces. Chop the onion.

3 Put the oil in a small saucepan on the hob. Turn the heat to medium. Add the onion to the oil in the pan and cook it, stirring occasionally, for about 5 minutes, or until it is soft but not brown. Stir in the sage and bread. Cook for 5 minutes, stirring all the time.

4 Add the baked beans to the bread mixture and heat them until they are boiling. Stir the beans occasionally.

5 Grate the cheese. Turn the heat off. Take the pan off the heat and stir in the cheese with a little salt and pepper.

6 Put the bread roll shells on plates and fill them with the bean mixture. Put the roll tops on top and serve at once. A crunchy salad tastes good with these.

▪►· toast toppers ·◄▪

Here are some ideas for hot toast toppings. Make the topping before you toast the bread so the toast does not go cold and hard.
★ Always take great care when using the grill. Use oven gloves to handle the grill pan. Before putting food under the grill have plates ready to put it on when it is cooked. Watch the food all the time it is cooking under the grill so it doesn't burn.
★ All these toppings are for 2 pieces of toast.

FISH-TOPPED FINGERS
Put 50 g/2 oz soft cheese in a basin. Add a small pot of salmon paste. Mix them together, then stir in 1 teaspoon tomato ketchup. Spread the mixture on the toast and cook it under the grill until hot. Cut the toast into fingers and top each one with parsley.

APPLE AND CHEESE
Wash and dry 1 dessert apple. Hold the apple at both ends of the core, then grate it on the coarse side of a grater. Grate all the flesh off the apple until you reach the core. Mix 50 g/2 oz grated cheese with the apple. Use a teaspoon to put the mixture all over the toast, then cook it under the grill until the cheese has melted.

PEANUT RAREBIT
In a basin mix 2 tablespoons crunchy peanut butter with 2 tablespoons milk. When the peanut butter is very soft mix in 50 g/2 oz grated cheese and add a little salt and pepper. Spread this over the toast. Cook under the grill until bubbling.

PIZZA TOPPING
In a small basin mix 25 g/1 oz softened butter or margarine with 1 tablespoon tomato purée and ¼ teaspoon dried marjoram. Mix in a little salt and pepper. Spread the tomato mixture on the toast. Top each slice of toast with a slice of cheese. Cook the cheese under the grill until bubbling.

▫►· Sesame Cheese puffs ·◄▫

75 g / 3 oz cheese
2 tablespoons sage and onion stuffing mix
plain flour for rolling out pastry
100 g / 4 oz puff pastry, thawed if frozen
a little milk or beaten egg
1 tablespoon sesame seeds

Makes 8

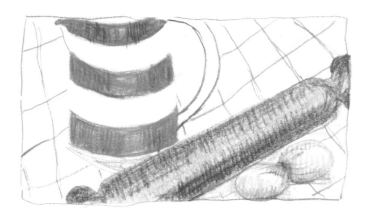

1 Grate the cheese. In a basin, mix the cheese with the stuffing mix. Set the oven at 230°C/450°F/gas 8. Have a baking tray ready – there is no need to grease it for these pastries.

2 Sprinkle a little flour on the work surface, then roll out the pastry into a 20 cm/8 in square. Only roll the pastry out away from you and do not press too hard. Press the edges of the pastry into shape with your fingers every now and then to make sure it stays square as you roll it.

3 Sprinkle the cheese mixture over half the pastry, leaving a narrow border all around the edge. Brush this border with a little water. Fold the other half of the pastry over the cheese filling and press it down firmly all over. Press the edges together.

4 Cut the pastry across into 2.5 cm/1 in wide strips. Press each strip together firmly to hold in the filling, then put them on the baking tray. Brush the top of each strip carefully with a little milk or egg. Sprinkle a few sesame seeds on top of each strip.

5 Bake the strips for 7–10 minutes. While they are baking, set out a wire rack and put a heatproof mat on the work surface. Open the oven to have a look. The pastry strips should be puffed up and golden brown. Turn the oven off. Use oven gloves to lift the baking tray from the oven. Take great care not to burn yourself.

6 Put the baking tray on the mat. Use a palette knife or fish slice to life the Sesame Cheese Puffs off the baking tray and put them on the wire rack to cool.

▸·crunchy hot orange·◂

2 chocolate chip cookies
1 orange
½ teaspoon honey
2 tablespoons
natural yogurt

Serves 2

1 Place the cookies in a polythene bag and use a rolling pin to crush them. Do not break them too much.

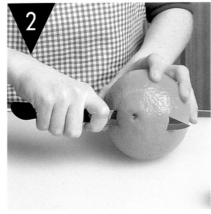

2 Cut a very small slice of peel off the top and bottom of the orange. Cut the orange in half.

3 Use a small knife to cut between the orange segments and cut all around the inside of the skin so that the fruit comes out easily.

4 Place the orange on a baking tray and spoon on a little honey. Put them under the grill for 2–3 minutes until they are hot.

5 Pile the crushed biscuits on top of the oranges.

6 Decorate each with a spoonful of yogurt.

▸· Simple Scones ·◂

225 g/8 oz plain flour
3 teaspoons baking powder
50 g/2 oz margarine
2 tablespoons caster sugar
150 ml/¼ pint milk
extra plain flour
milk for brushing

Makes 12

DIFFERENT SORTS OF SCONES

★ Add 50 g/2 oz sultanas or raisins with the sugar.
★ Add 50 g/2 oz chopped walnuts with the sugar.
★ Do not add the sugar. Instead, add 50 g/2 oz grated cheese after you have rubbed in the margarine to make Cheese Scones.
★ Do not add the sugar. Instead, add 50 g/2 oz grated cheese and ½ teaspoon dried mixed herbs after you have rubbed in the margarine to make Cheese and Herb Scones.
★ Scones with cheese added may have a little grated cheese sprinkled on top before baking.

1 Set the oven at 220°C/425°F/gas 7. Grease a baking tray. Put the flour in a bowl and stir in the baking powder. Add the margarine. Rub the fat into the flour until the mixture resembles fine breadcrumbs.

2 Stir in the sugar. Make a well in the middle of the mixture. Pour the milk into the well and stir the flour into it until you have a soft dough.

3 Sprinkle some flour on the work surface and turn the dough on to it. Sprinkle just a little flour on your fingers, then gently knead the dough into a ball.

4 Use a rolling pin sprinkled with a little flour to roll the dough out until it is 1.5 cm/¾ in thick. Use a round pastry cutter measuring about 5 cm/2 in across. Dip it in a little flour, then cut out rounds of dough. Gather up all the scraps of dough and roll them out to cut out more scones.

5 Put the scones on the baking tray. Brush their tops with a little milk and bake them for 7–10 minutes. While they are cooking put a wire rack ready. Put a heatproof mat on the work surface.

6 Turn off the heat. Use oven gloves to take the scones from the oven, then use a fish slice to lift them on to the rack. Eat the scones warm, with some butter and jam.

ɪ▸· orange flapjacks ·◂ɪ

1 orange
100 g/4 oz margarine
4 tablespoons golden syrup
2 tablespoons demerara sugar
225 g/8 oz rolled oats

Makes 16

1 Set the oven at 190°C/375°F/gas 5. Grease a 20 cm/8 in square tin really well. Grate the rind from the orange and put it in a small saucepan.

2 Add the margarine and syrup to the orange rind. Put the saucepan on the hob and turn the heat to medium. Stir the mixture in the pan until all the butter has melted. Turn the heat off.

3 Put the rolled oats in a bowl. Pour the melted mixture over the oats and mix them really well. Turn the mixture into the tin and press it down firmly until the top is smooth and even.

4 Bake the mixture for 30–35 minutes, until it is golden brown and firm. Put a heatproof mat on the work surface. Use oven gloves to remove the flapjacks from the oven.

5 Leave the mixture in the tin on the mat. When it is just warm, cut it into 16 square pieces. Leave them in the tin until they are cold and firm. Use a palette knife to remove the flapjacks.

ɪ▸· brownies ·◂ɪ

1 Set the oven at 180°C/350°F/gas 4. Lay a piece of greaseproof paper on the work surface and stand a 20 cm/8 in square tin on it. Use a pencil to draw around the bottom of the tin. Cut out the paper along your pencil line. Grease the tin well. Put the square of paper in the bottom of the tin, then grease the paper.

2 Put the flour, cocoa, baking powder and sugar in a bowl and mix well. Add the margarine, eggs and vanilla essence. Stir all the ingredients into a smooth, soft mixture. Use a spoon to put the mixture into the tin and scrape the bowl clean. Spread the mixture out evenly.

3 Bake the Brownies for 40–45 minutes, until risen and the edges have come away from the tin. Put a heatproof mat on the work surface. Use oven gloves to remove the tin from the oven. Leave the Brownies in the tin on the mat until cold. Cut into 16 squares.

75 g/3 oz self-raising flour
25 g/1 oz cocoa powder
½ teaspoon baking powder
100 g/4 oz soft brown sugar
75 g/3 oz soft margarine
2 eggs
1 teaspoon vanilla essence

Makes 16

▶·banana muffins·◀

100 g/4 oz plain flour
2 teaspoons baking powder
50 g/2 oz sugar
25 g/1oz raisins
1 banana
25 g/1 oz soft margarine
1 egg
6 tablespoons milk

Makes 9

MUFFIN MANIA

You can add other ingredients to banana muffins:
* ★ *Add 50 g/2 oz roughly chopped walnuts.*
* ★ *Add 25 g/1 oz chopped ready-to-eat dried apricots.*
* ★ *Add 2 tablespoons peanut butter with the margarine.*

1 Set the oven at 200°C/400°F/gas 6. Grease 9 deep muffin tins or put 9 deep paper cake cases in patty tins. Mix the flour, baking powder, sugar and raisins in a bowl.

2 Peel the banana, break it into pieces and put them in a basin. Mash the banana with a fork until it is smooth, then add it to the dry ingredients.

3 Add the margarine and egg. Use a wooden spoon to mix all the ingredients. Add about half the milk and beat well. Beat in the remaining milk.

4 Use a teaspoon to put the mixture into the tins or paper cases, dividing it evenly. Bake the muffins for 20–25 minutes, until they are risen and golden brown. They will rise into peaks and crack slightly.

5 While the muffins are cooking, get out a wire rack and put a heatproof mat on the work surface. Turn off the heat. Use oven gloves to remove the muffins. Use a palette knife to take the muffins from their tins. Leave them to cool and eat them while they are warm.

REAL MEALS

Menu
Pronto Pasta
Exotic Jelly

1 Make the Exotic Jelly several hours before the meal or make it the day before.
2 Prepare all the ingredients for the pasta.
3 Cook the pasta and mix it with the ingredients when you are ready to eat.

▶·*pronto pasta*·◀

1 onion
2 tablespoons vegetable oil
100 g/4 oz mushrooms
½ teaspoon dried mixed herbs
400 g/14 oz can choppped tomatoes
salt and pepper
4 frankfurters
350 g/12 oz pasta shapes
50 g/2 oz cheese
2 tablespoons chopped parsley

Serves 4

1 Peel and chop the onion. Put the oil in a saucepan over medium heat. Add the onion and cook, stirring occasionally, for about 10 minutes. The onion should be very soft but not browned.

2 While the onion is cooking, cut the end off each mushroom stalk. Rinse the mushrooms under running water, holding the round top up. Rub off any dirt. Slice the mushrooms. Add them to the onion and stir in the dried herbs. Add the tomatoes and bring the mixture to the boil. Sprinkle a little salt and pepper into the sauce. Turn the heat to the lowest setting. Slice the frankfurters and stir them into the sauce. Continue cooking, uncovered, and stir once in a while.

3 Grate the cheese and set aside.

4 You will need a large saucepan full of water to cook the pasta. Put it on the hob. Add a little salt and bring the water to the boil. When the water is boiling add the pasta. Stir the pasta once. Bring the water back to the boil but be ready to turn the heat down so that it does not boil over. The pasta should boil without frothing over the edge of the pan. Cook it like this for 15 minutes.

5 Put a colander in the sink. Turn the heat off. Use oven gloves and lift the pan of pasta from the hob, then turn it into the colander to drain. Put the pasta in a large dish. Turn the heat off under the sauce, then stir it and pour it over the pasta. Sprinkle with the cheese and parsley and serve at once. Use a spoon and fork to mix the pasta and sauce together before putting it on to plates.

ORDER OF WORK

1 Make the Chocolate Yogurt Swirl in advance and put it in the refrigerator.
2 Collect all the ingredients for the pizza and for the salad. Wash the salad ingredients and set them aside in the refrigerator so they stay crisp.
3 Make the pizza.
4 Make the salad while the pizza is baking.

▶·*p*izza·◀

1 onion
1 green pepper
2 tablespoons vegetable oil
4 tablespoons tomato purée
1 teaspoon dried marjoram
salt and pepper
100 g / 4 oz self-raising flour
25 g / 1 oz margarine
50 ml / 2 fl oz milk
a little flour
50 g / 2 oz frozen sweetcorn, peas or mixed vegetables
100 g / 4 oz cheese
50 g / 2 oz cooked ham

Serves 4

1 Peel and chop the onion. Cut the green pepper in half. Use a small pointed knife to cut out all the seeds and the core from each half. Cut off all the stalk from each half. Cut 1 piece of pepper into long strips, then hold all the strips together and cut across them to make small dice. Repeat with the other half.

2 Put the oil in a small saucepan. Put it on the hob and turn the heat to medium. Add the onion and diced pepper after a few seconds. Cook, stirring, for 5 minutes. Take it off the heat. Stir in the tomato purée, dried marjoram and a little seasoning. Leave to cool.

3 Grease a baking tray. Set the oven at 220°C/425°F/gas 7. Put the flour in a bowl and add the margarine. Cut the margarine into small pieces. Wash your hands, then rub the fat into the flour. Mix in the milk to make a dough and press it together with your fingers.

4 Put a little flour on the work surface and turn the dough on to it. Knead it lightly into a smooth ball. Put a little flour on a rolling pin, then roll out the dough into a circle about 20 cm/8 in across. Put the rolling pin near the middle of the dough, then fold the dough over it. Use the rolling pin to lift to the baking tray. Spread the onion mixture over the dough, leaving a small border all around the edge. Sprinkle the vegetables over the onion. Grate the cheese on the coarse side of the grater, then sprinkle it over the vegetables.

5 Cut the ham into thin strips. Place the strips in a crisscross pattern across the top of the pizza. Bake the pizza for about 15 minutes, until it is risen, bubbling and golden on top. Put a heatproof mat on the work surface. Turn the heat off. Use oven gloves to take the pizza from the oven. Cut it into wedges to serve.

▶· Salad Spectacular ·◀

2 carrots
2 sticks celery
4 spring onions
4 tomatoes
1 courgette
1 lettuce heart
2 tablespoons olive or sunflower oil
1 tablespoon lemon juice

Serves 4

1 Peel the carrots and cut off their ends. Grate them on the coarse side of the grater. Put them on a plate. Wash the celery and use a brush to scrub all the dirt from inside the sticks. Cut across the sticks to make thin slices. Put the celery beside the carrots on the plate, keeping both separate.

2 Wash and trim the ends off the spring onions. Peel away any bad bits. Cut the onions across into small pieces. Push them to one side of the board or put them on a plate. Cut the tomatoes into quarters.

3 Wash and dry the courgette. Cut off the ends, then cut the courgette in half lengthways. Put the cut side of a half down on the board, then cut it into thin slices. Slice the other half in the same way.

SALAD IDEAS

You can use different vegetables to make this salad. Make sure they are all cut up into small, neat pieces. Try white or red cabbage, cucumber, watercress, mushrooms or cauliflower. Add some crunchy beansprouts, too.

4 Wash and dry the lettuce. Use your fingers to tear the leaves into small pieces. You will need a large platter for the salad. Arrange all the vegetables in neat mounds coming from the centre of the platter out to the edge. Very carefully trickle the oil all over the salad, then trickle the lemon juice over.

▶· Chocolate Yogurt Swirl ·◀

100 g / 4 oz chocolate
25 g / 1 oz butter
2 tablespoons golden syrup
4 150 g / 5 oz pots of fruit yogurt or 1 450 g / 1 lb tub
2 tablespoons chopped nuts

Serves 4

1 Break the chocolate into squares and put them in a heatproof basin. Add the butter and the syrup. Pour some water into a small saucepan and put it on the hob over medium heat. Stand the basin in the pan over the water. Heat the mixture until the chocolate melts, stirring occasionally. Make sure that the water does not boil up underneath the basin. Turn the heat down to low if the water begins to boil.

2 Turn the heat off and use a tea-towel or oven gloves to lift the basin off the water. Set the chocolate mixture aside until it is cool. Pour the yogurt into 4 dishes. Use a spoon to swirl the chocolate mixture through the yogurt. Put the dishes in the refrigerator until you are ready to serve them. Sprinkle the nuts over the top of the yogurt just before serving.

Menu
Pork 'n' Potato Loaf
Stir-fry Vegetables
Banana Splits

ORDER OF WORK

1 Make the jam sauce for the Banana Splits.
2 Make the Pork 'n' Potato Loaf.
3 Prepare the vegetables while the Pork 'n' Potato Loaf is cooking.
4 Stir-fry the vegetables as soon as the Pork 'n' Potato Loaf is removed from the oven.
5 Make the Banana Splits just before you are ready to eat them.

·▶·pork 'n' potato loaf·◀·

1 You will need a 500 g/1 lb loaf tin and a piece of greaseproof paper. Stand the tin on the paper and draw all around it with a pencil. Cut out the shape. Grease the tin and put the paper in it. Grease the paper. Set the oven at 190°C/375°F/gas 5.

2 Put the meat in a bowl. Peel the onion, then grate it on the coarse side of the grater. Take care not to grate your fingers. Cut the last little piece up very small. Add the onion to the meat. Mix in the sage with plenty of salt and pepper. Break 1 egg into a cup, then tip it into the basin and mix it well with the meat.

3 Peel the potatoes. Wash and dry them. Grate them on the coarse side of the grater. Squeeze the grated potato, then put it in another basin. Break the second egg into a cup, then tip it into the potato. Add the flour and plenty of salt and pepper. Mix well.

4 Put half the potato mixture into the tin and press it down with the back of a spoon. Put all the meat mixture on top, pressing it down so that it is smooth. Put the remaining potato mixture into the tin and spread it out evenly. Bake the loaf for 1¼ hours, until it is brown and crisp on top.

5 Have a heatproof mat ready for the tin. Use oven gloves to remove the tin from the oven. Turn the oven off. Put a plate upside down on the tin. Use oven gloves to hold them, then turn the tin upside down on to the plate. Lift the tin off. Peel the paper off the loaf.

6 Cut the tomato into slices and arrange them on top of the loaf. Add some parsley sprigs. Cut the loaf into slices to serve.

500 g/1 lb lean minced pork
1 onion
1 teaspoon dried sage
salt and pepper
2 small eggs
500 g/1 lb potatoes
4 tablespoons plain flour
1 tomato
a few parsley sprigs

Serves 4

▶·Stir-fry Vegetables·◀

1 leek
4 sticks celery
1 red pepper
225 g/8 oz green cabbage
3 tablespoons vegetable oil
salt and pepper

Serves 4

HELP POINT
Turning hot food out on to a serving plate is difficult so always ask an adult to help.

Trim the ends off the leek. Cut in half lengthways, then wash both pieces under cold running water to get rid of all the grit. Drain off the water, then cut both pieces into thin slices. **1**

Wash the celery, scrubbing off all the dirt. Cut the sticks into thin slices. Cut the pepper in half. Cut out the stalk and the core with all the seeds. Rinse both halves under running water. Cut the pieces in half lengthways, then across into short thin strips. **2**

Cut any large pieces of stalk from the cabbage. Cut across the leaves to give fine slices that fall into shreds as they are cut. Put the cabbage in a colander and wash it under cold water. Leave to drain. **3**

Put the oil in a large frying pan or wok. Put it on the hob and turn the heat to high. Add the leeks, celery and red pepper. Cook the vegetables for 3 minutes, stirring all the time. **4**

Add the cabbage and sprinkle in a little salt and pepper. Continue stirring the vegetables. Reduce the heat to medium and cook for another 5 minutes, stirring all the time. Turn off the heat and serve at once. **5**

STIR-FRY SPECIALS

Lots of different vegetables may be stir-fried. Try sliced onion, small baby sweet corn, sliced French beans, beansprouts, small pieces of cauliflower, sliced Brussels sprouts, sliced spring onions or mushrooms.

▶·banana splits·◀

100 g/4 oz jam
3 tablespoons orange juice
4 small bananas
8 small scoops vanilla ice cream
8–12 strawberries (optional)

Serves 4

1 Put the jam in a basin. Pour some water into a small saucepan and put it on the hob. Stand the basin over the water and turn the heat to medium. Stir the jam until it has melted. Turn the heat off and use oven gloves to lift the basin off the saucepan.

2 Stir the orange juice into the jam, then leave it until cold. Peel the bananas and cut them in half lengthways. Put the 2 halves slightly apart on plates.

3 Put 2 scoops of ice cream between each pair of banana halves. Use a teaspoon to trickle the jam sauce over the top. Add 2 or 3 strawberries to each Banana Split if you like and serve at once.

ORDER OF WORK
1 Make the Rice Cocktails and put them in the refrigerator.
2 Make the Fish Finger Flan.
3 Heat the baked beans 5 minutes before the end of the cooking time for the flan.

▶ fish finger flan ◀

175 g/6 oz plain flour
75 g/3 oz margarine
1–2 tablespoons cold water
75 g/3 oz cheese
4 spring onions
2 eggs
150 ml/¼ pint milk
salt and pepper
6 frozen fish fingers
parsley sprig

Serves 6

1 Set the oven at 190°C/375°F/gas 5. Put the flour in a basin. Add the margarine and cut it into small pieces. Using just the tips of your fingers, rub the fat into the flour. Lift the fat and flour as you rub them together, then let the bits fall back into the basin. The mixture is ready when it looks like fine breadcrumbs.

2 Add 1 tablespoon cold water and mix the pastry with a knife. If it does not form large lumps add the rest of the water. Press the pastry together into a ball.

3 Get out a 20 cm/8 in flan dish. Put a little flour on the work surface and on your rolling pin. Roll out the pastry into a circle large enough to line the flan dish. To measure the pastry, hold the dish over it. There should be enough all around the edge to come up the side of the dish.

4 Put the rolling pin on the pastry. Fold the pastry over the pin, then use the rolling pin to lift it into the flan dish. Press the pastry down into the dish. If you have any breaks in the pastry just press them together with your fingers. Roll the rolling pin over the top of the dish to cut off the extra pastry.

5 Prick the pastry all over with a fork. Put a sheet of greaseproof paper in the flan. Sprinkle some dried peas over the paper. Bake the pastry for 10 minutes. Put a heatproof mat on the work surface. Use oven gloves to lift the dish from the oven. Lift the peas and paper out of the pastry case. Reduce the oven temperature to 180°C/350°F/gas 4.

6 Grate the cheese. Cut any bad bits off the spring onions, then wash them and cut them across into small pieces. Beat the eggs with the milk, adding a little salt and pepper. Set aside.

7 Sprinkle the cheese all over the bottom of the flan. Scatter the spring onions over the cheese, then pour in the eggs and milk. Arrange the fish fingers in the flan like the spokes of a wheel. Bake the flan for 50–60 minutes, or until the top of the fish fingers are brown and crisp and the egg is set.

Have a heatproof mat ready to put the flan on. Use oven gloves to lift the dish from the oven. Turn the oven off. Place a sprig of parsley in the middle of the flan and serve cut wedges. This can be served hot or at room temperature.

▸· baked beans ·◂

425 g/15 oz can baked beans

Serves 4

1 Get out a small saucepan. Open the can of beans and pour them into the pan. Put the pan on the hob and turn the heat to medium.

2 Stir the beans occasionally until they are just boiling and hot through. Turn off the heat. Serve with the Fish Finger Flan.

BEANS ON TOAST

To make Beans on Toast, toast 4 slices of bread on both sides while the beans are heating. Spread some butter or margarine on the toast, then put the slices on plates. Spoon the beans over the toast and serve at once.

▸· rice cocktails ·◂

50 g/2 oz glacé cherries
25 g/1 oz raisins
298 g/10½ oz can mandarin oranges
small piece angelica
425 g/15 oz can creamed rice pudding

Serves 4

1 Cut the cherries into quarters and put them in a small basin with the raisins. Open the can of mandarin oranges. Hold the lid in place and drain all the juice from the can into another basin. Add 2 tablespoons of the juice to the cherries and raisins. The rest of the juice may be used to make a drink.

2 Leave the cherries and raisins to soak for 30 minutes. Cut the angelica into small pieces. Open the rice pudding and put it in a bowl.

3 Add the mandarin oranges and angelica to the rice. Pour in the cherries and raisins and stir well. Divide the Rice Cocktails between 4 glass bowls. Put in the refrigerator for at least 30 minutes.

Menu
Pastacular
No-cook Chocolate Fudge Flan

ORDER OF WORK
1 Make the No-cook Chocolate Fudge Flan several hours before the meal so it has time to set.
2 Prepare all the ingredients for the pasta dish at least 1 hour before you intend to serve the meal.

▸·*p*astacular·◂

1 Trim the ends off the mushroom stalks. Rinse the mushrooms, wiping off any bits of dirt. Dry them on absorbent kitchen paper, then slice them.

2 Remove the rind from the sausage if necessary. Cut the sausage into fairly thin slices. Grate the cheese. Peel and chop the onion.

3 Three-quarters fill a large saucepan with water and put it on the hob. Add a little salt and turn the heat to high. When the water boils add the pasta and give it a stir. Stand by to turn the heat down to medium as soon as the water boils. If you leave the heat on high the water will boil over. Boil the pasta for 15 minutes. Put a colander in the sink. Turn the heat off and pour the pasta into the colander. Leave to drain.

4 Put the butter in a medium saucepan and put it on the hob. Turn the heat to medium. Add the onion to the butter and cook, stirring, for 5 minutes.

5 Add the flour to the onion and stir to make a paste. Slowly pour the milk into the pan, stirring all the time. Stir in the frozen beans. Keep stirring until the sauce boils and thickens. Once it has boiled, cook the sauce for 3 minutes.

6 Add the mushrooms to the sauce and stir in the cheese. Sprinkle in a little salt and pepper. Cook, stirring, until the cheese has melted. Do not let it boil. Taste the sauce to check whether it has enough seasoning.

7 Add the cooked pasta to the sauce, stir well and cook gently for about 5 minutes, until it is hot. The beans should be hot and lightly cooked, with a bit of crunch.

8 Heat the grill. Turn the pasta mixture into a flameproof serving dish and put it under the grill until golden brown on top. Have a heatproof mat ready. Use oven gloves to remove the dish from under the grill. Turn the heat off.

100 g/4 oz mushrooms
350 g/12 oz smoked sausage
50 g/2 oz cheese
1 onion
225 g/8 oz pasta spirals
25 g/1 oz butter
40 g/1½ oz plain flour
600 ml/1 pint milk
salt and pepper
100 g/4 oz frozen cut green beans

Serves 4

▶·no-cook chocolate fudge flan·◀

100 g/4 oz plain sweet biscuits
50 g/2 oz butter

Filling
175 g/6 oz plain cake
175 g/6 oz plain chocolate
50 g/2 oz butter
6 tablespoons golden syrup
1 tablespoon cocoa powder
100 g/4 oz cream cheese
2 tablespoons icing sugar
2 tablespoons orange juice

Serves 4–6

1 Put the biscuits in a polythene bag. Twist the end closed, then fold it over. Use a rolling pin to crush the biscuits, taking care not to break the bag.

2 Put the butter in a medium saucepan. Put the pan on the hob and turn the heat to medium. When the butter has melted, turn the heat off and tip all the biscuits into the butter. Stir well.

3 Turn the buttered biscuits into a 15 cm/6 in flan dish. Press them all over the base and up the side of the dish in a thin, even coating. Put the dish in the refrigerator to chill the biscuit mixture.

4 Put the cake in a bowl. Wash and dry your hands. Crumble the cake into small, even pieces.

5 Break the chocolate into squares and put it in a saucepan. Add the butter, syrup and cocoa. Put the pan on the hob and turn the heat to low. Stir the mixture until the butter has melted and the golden syrup is runny. Turn the heat off.

6 Pour the chocolate mixture over the cake crumbs and mix really well. Carry on mixing until every bit of cake has absorbed the chocolate. Put the chocolate cake mixture into the biscuit case and press it down evenly.

7 Put the cheese in a bowl with the icing sugar and the orange juice. Beat well until the cheese is very soft. Pile this on top of the flan and swirl it out evenly.

8 Chill the flan for at least 1 hour before serving it cut into wedges.

FAST FOODS

frankfurter kebabs

2 frankfurters
4 small tomatoes
8 button mushrooms
a little oil
salt and pepper

Mustard Sauce
1 tablespoon French mustard
4 tablespoons natural yogurt or fromage frais
1 spring onion

1 Cut each frankfurter into 4 pieces. Cut the tomatoes in half. Thread 4 pieces of frankfurter, 4 mushrooms and 4 tomato halves on a long metal skewer. Thread the rest of the ingredients on another metal skewer.

2 Mix the mustard with the fromage frais or yogurt. Trim the ends off the spring onion. Wash and dry it on absorbent kitchen paper, then cut it into small pieces. Stir the spring onion into the sauce.

3 Heat the grill. Brush a little oil over the kebabs and sprinkle with a little salt and pepper. Put the kebabs under the grill for 3 minutes. Use oven gloves to hold the end of the skewers and turn the kebabs over. Cook for another 3 minutes.

4 Serve the mustard sauce with the kebabs.

SERVING IDEAS

★ Have pitta bread with the kebabs. Warm the pitta at the bottom of the grill while you cook the kebabs. Split the bread down one side and fill it with the food off the skewers.
★ Arrange the kebabs on a plate of shredded lettuce.
★ Serve Coleslaw Cups with the kebabs.
★ Heat a small can of baked beans or spaghetti in tomato sauce to go with the kebabs.

⊩•·burger salad·◂⊩

1 eating apple
1 small carrot
1 spring onion
salt and pepper
1 long Granary roll
2 lettuce leaves
1 frozen burger
4 slices cucumber

Serves 1

MICROWAVE METHOD

★ *Check the weight of the burger. Put it on a plate.*
★ *Cook on Full Power. Allow about 1½–2 minutes for a 50 g/2 oz burger. A 100 g/4 oz burger takes about 3–3½ minutes.*

1 Peel the apple. Grate all the flesh off the core on the coarse side of the grater. Put the grated apple in a basin.

2 Peel the carrot and trim off the ends. Grate it on the coarse side of the grater. Mix the carrot with the apple. Trim any bad bits off the spring onion. Wash and dry it. Cut it across into small pieces. Mix the spring onion with the salad, adding a little salt and pepper.

3 Split the roll lengthways without cutting it right through. Wash and dry the lettuce leaves. Put them in the roll. Put the salad in the roll. Heat the grill.

4 Cook the burger under the grill for 3–5 minutes. It should be well browned. Use a fish slice and a fork to turn the burger over. Cook the second side for 3–5 minutes. Turn the heat off.

5 Cut the burger across the middle in half. Put the pieces onto the salad in the roll. Add the cucumber slices.

▶· tuna rarebit rolls ·◀

99 g / 3½ oz can tuna
50 g / 2 oz cheese
2 tablespoons milk
salt and pepper
2 round bread rolls
about 8 slices cucumber
4 parsley sprigs

Serves 2

1 Spread the tuna mixture thickly over the half-toasted rolls. Put them back under the grill until the topping is brown. Turn the heat off.

2 Put the rolls on plates and top each half with cucumber slices and a sprig of parsley. Take care when eating – the topping is very hot!

3 Drain the liquid from the tuna. Put the tuna in a basin. Grate the cheese and mix it with the tuna. Add the milk. Sprinkle in some salt and pepper.

4 Mix the ingredients really well so they combine to make a thick paste.

5 Heat the grill. Slice the rolls in half through the middle. Put the rolls on the rack with the cut sides down. Cook until the tops are golden. Turn the rolls over. Cook the cut sides until they are only lightly browned.

▶· toasted sandwich ·◀

1 Heat the grill. Spread a little butter or margarine on the bread slices. Sandwich the bread and cheese together, pressing them down firmly, with the unbuttered sides of the bread on the outside.

2 Put the sandwich under the grill until it is golden brown on one side. Turn the sandwich over and toast the second side. Turn the grill off and eat the sandwich while it is hot. Take care when you bite the filling – the cheese gets very hot!

TREMENDOUS TOASTED SANDWICHES

Try these fillings.
★ Cheese, thinly sliced apples and a little chopped onion.
★ Mashed canned sardines with sliced pickled cucumber.
★ Mashed tuna fish with cottage cheese.
★ A thin slice of corned beef and a spoonful of baked beans.
★ A slice of cooked turkey with 2 teaspoons of cranberry sauce.
★ A slice of cooked pork with 2 teaspoons apple sauce.
★ A cooked bacon rasher with a sliced tomato.
★ Peanut butter with sliced frankfurter.

SANDWICH TOASTERS

If you have a special electric sandwich toaster ask an adult to show you how to use it. The toaster should be heated up before the sandwiches are put in it, then they are cooked for about 3 minutes. They will be very hot.

▸ Sandwich rolls ◂   ▸ pizza sticks ◂

100 g/4 oz plain flour
50 g/2 oz margarine
½ teaspoon dried marjoram
50 g/2 oz cheese
salt and pepper
1 teaspoon tomato purée
1 tablespoon water
extra plain flour
beaten egg or milk, to glaze

Makes 12

3 eggs
2 tablespoons mayonnaise
50 g/2 oz cheese
salt and pepper
12 large, thin slices bread

Makes 24

Set the oven at 200°C/400°F/gas 6. Grease a baking tray. Sprinkle a little flour on the work surface, then gently knead the dough until smooth. Flatten it into a big sausage, then cut this into 12 equal pieces. Roll the pieces of dough into thin sticks measuring about 15cm/6 in long.

Put the dough sticks on the greased baking tray, leaving a little room between them. Brush them with a little beaten egg or milk. Bake for 15–20 minutes, until the sticks are golden brown.

1 Put the eggs in a small saucepan and pour in enough cold water to cover them. Put the pan on the hob and turn the heat to high. As soon as the water boils, turn the heat down to medium. Boil the eggs for 10 minutes. Turn the heat off. Pour off most of the boiling water down the sink. Run cold water over the eggs in the pan, then leave them to cool.

While the sticks are baking, set out a wire rack to put them on. Put a heatproof mat on the work surface. Turn off the heat. Use oven gloves to take the baking tray from the oven. Use a palette knife or slice to lift the pizza sticks off the tray and put them on the wire rack to cool.

2 Crack the eggs and peel off the shells. Put them in a basin and mash them with a fork until they are very fine. Stir in the mayonnaise. Grate the cheese and mix it into the eggs with some salt and pepper.

Put the flour in a bowl. Add the margarine, then use a knife to cut the margarine into small pieces. Rub the fat into the flour.

3 Cut the crusts off the bread. Spread a slice with some of the egg mixture. Roll it up from the short side, pressing it firmly together without squeezing out the filling. If the bread will not stay rolled, put 2 cocktail sticks through it. Cut the roll in half.

Add the marjoram. Grate the cheese on the coarse side of the grater and add it to the mixture. Stir in some salt and pepper. In a mug or small basin, mix the tomato purée with the water, then add the mixture to the dry ingredients. Use a palette knife or a blunt knife to mix the ingredients together. When the mixture forms large lumps, use your fingers to press it together into a ball.

4 Make all the other rolls, then pack them close together in a container or in cling film. The cocktail sticks may be removed when the sandwiches are packed.

▶ basic biscuits ◀

225 g/8 oz plain flour
½ teaspoon baking powder
100 g/4 oz butter or margarine
40 g/1½ oz icing sugar
2 egg yolks
1 teaspoon vanilla essence

Makes 30–35

1

Set the oven at 180°C/350°F/gas 4. Grease 2 baking trays. Put the flour and baking powder in a bowl. Add the butter or margarine and cut it into small pieces. Use your fingertips to rub the fat into the flour. The mixture is ready when it looks like breadcrumbs.

2

Stir in the icing sugar. Make a well in the middle of the mixture. Put in the egg yolk and vanilla essence. Stir the egg and vanilla into the rubbed in mixture until it forms clumps. Then use your fingers to press the mixture together into a dough.

3

Cut the dough in half. Put a little flour on the work surface and on your rolling pin. Knead 1 piece of dough into a smooth flat round, then roll it out to about 5 mm/¼ in thick. Use cutters to cut out the biscuits.

4

Cut the biscuits in all sorts of different shapes. Re-roll all the trimmings. Repeat with the second portion of dough.

5

Put the biscuits on the baking trays. Bake for about 15 minutes, until lightly browned.

6

Use oven gloves to take the trays from the oven. Turn off the heat. Use a palette knife to lift the biscuits off the trays. Put them on the wire rack to cool. Add toppings and decorations to the cold biscuits.

TOPPINGS

★ Melted chocolate with chopped nuts.
★ Glacé icing. Follow the instructions for making the icing used on Clever Cookies . Top the biscuits with halved cherries or chocolate polka dots.
★ Melt 2 tablespoons crunchy peanut butter with 100 g/4 oz chocolate.
★ Orange icing – mix 100 g/4 oz icing sugar with 1–2 tablespoons orange juice.

DIFFERENT FLAVOURED BISCUITS

Chocolate – add 2 tablespoons cocoa powder with the icing sugar.
St Clement's – add the grated rind of 1 lemon and 1 orange with the icing sugar.
Walnut – add 50 g/2 oz finely chopped walnuts with the icing sugar.
Chocolate Chip – stick chocolate polka dots into the cookies before baking them.

DECORATIONS

★ Coloured sugar strands or chocolate strands
★ Chocolate buttons, milk and white
★ Small jellied sweets
★ Silver balls
★ Mimosa balls
★ Halved or quartered glacé cherries with strips of angelica
★ Flaked almonds

▷·peanut cookies ·◁

75 g/3 oz soft margarine
75 g/3 oz soft light brown sugar
1 teaspoon vanilla essence
100 g/4 oz self-raising flour
75 g/3 oz salted peanuts

Makes about 15

1 Set the oven at 180°C/350°F/gas 4. Grease 2 baking trays. Put the margarine in a bowl with the sugar. Beat well until the mixture is very soft and light.

2 Stir in the vanilla essence. Add all the flour and the peanuts. Mix well until all the ingredients are combined. The mixture will make a soft dough.

3 Take small lumps of the dough and roll them into balls about the size of walnuts. Place the balls well apart on the baking trays. Flatten the balls with a fork. Bake for about 15 minutes, until golden.

4 Put out a wire rack. Use oven gloves to remove the trays from the oven. Have a heatproof mat ready. Turn off the heat. Leave the cookies on the trays for 2 minutes, then use a palette knife to put them on the wire rack. Leave until cold.

▸·Stuffed tomatoes·◂

2 eggs
6 medium tomatoes
50 g/2 oz fresh breadcrumbs
2 tablespoons snipped chives
2 tablespoons chopped parsley
parsley sprigs, to garnish

Makes 6

Boil your eggs and shell them in a small basin and mash well.

when they are cool. Put them

Cut a thin slice off the top and chop into small pieces. Scoop out the soft middle, putting it all in a basin.

Drain the tomatoes upside down on kitchen paper. Add the breadcrumbs, chives and parsley to the basin.

Mix well, sprinkling in some salt and pepper.

Mix in the mashed egg with the tomato and breadcrumb mixture.

Use a teaspoon. Arrange the stuffed tomatoes on a plate. Garnish with parsley sprigs.

▶·garlic bread·◀

50 g/2 oz butter
1 small clove garlic
1 tablespoon chopped parsley
1 short French loaf

Makes 10 pieces

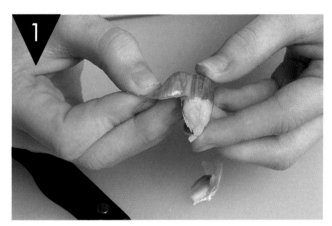

Set the oven at 200°C/400°F/gas 6. Put the butter in a small basin and soften it by creaming it with the back of a wooden spoon. Peel the garlic and put the clove in a garlic crusher.

Crush the garlic into the butter, scraping all the bits off the crusher. Add the parsley and mix well.

Cut the loaf into 10 slices. Lay a piece of foil, large enough to wrap the loaf, on the work surface. Spread the butter thinly on the slices and press them all back together on the piece of foil. Fold the foil around the loaf, pinching the edges together to seal the packet.

Put the bread in the oven for 10–15 minutes, until all the butter has melted and the bread is hot and crisp. Have a basket ready and put some absorbent kitchen paper or a napkin in it. Use oven gloves to remove the bread from the oven. Turn the heat off. Open the foil very carefully as steam will come out. Put the bread in the basket and serve at once.

▸ lemon jelly cheesecake ◂

Put the biscuits in a polythene bag. Twist the end of the bag closed but do not seal it. Use a rolling pin to crush the biscuits in the bag. Do this fairly gently so as not to break the bag. *1*

Put the butter in a medium saucepan. Put the pan on the hob and turn the heat to medium. When the butter has melted, turn the heat off. Add the biscuits to the butter and stir. Turn the biscuits into a 23 cm/9 in flan dish. Scrape all the bits from the saucepan. Press the biscuits evenly over the base of the dish. Put the dish in the refrigerator. *2*

Break the jelly into squares and put them in a basin. Pour the boiling water over the jelly. Stir until the cubes have dissolved completely. Leave until cold, then put the jelly in the refrigerator until it is just beginning to set. It should be rather like syrup. *3*

Put the cheese in a bowl. Add a little jelly and beat well. Gradually beat in all the jelly. Turn this mixture into the flan dish. Spread it evenly over the biscuit base. Put the cheesecake in the refrigerator until it is set. *4*

Turn the cream into a basin and use a whisk to whip it until it is thick enough to stand up in soft peaks. Put a star piping nozzle in a piping bag. Put the nozzle and the bag in a measuring jug, folding the ends of the bag over the outside of the jug. Spoon the cream into the bag, scraping every little bit out of the basin. *5*

Gather up the ends of the piping bag and twist them together. Hold the nozzle near the edge of the cheese-cake and squeeze out some cream. At the same time gently move the bag round to pipe a swirl. Pipe swirls all around the edge of the cheesecake. Put chocolate buttons between the swirls. Cut the cheesecake into wedges to serve. *6*

100 g/4 oz plain sweet biscuits
50 g/2 oz butter
1 lemon jelly tablet
300 ml/½ pint boiling water
500 g/1 lb cream cheese
150 ml/¼ pint double cream
chocolate buttons, to decorate

Serves 12

ham triangles

50 g/2 oz butter or margarine
8 thin slices bread
a little mustard
8 slices cooked ham
mustard and cress, to garnish

Makes 16

1 Place the butter in a basin and soften with a spoon. Cut the crusts off the bread and spread with butter.

2 Spread 4 slices with a little mustard. Place a slice of ham on top, then put the remaining bread on top, buttered sides down, to make sandwiches.

3 Cut the sandwiches across into 4 triangles. Arrange these on a plate and cover with cling film until you are ready to serve them. Put a few small bunches of mustard and cress around the sandwiches for garnish.

Stuffed Cucumber

20 cm/8 in piece cucumber
50 g/2 oz soft cheese with garlic and herbs
50 g/2 oz cooked ham or boneless chicken
8 parsley sprigs

Makes 8 pieces

1 Peel the cucumber. Cut it into 8 slices measuring 2.5 cm/1 in thick. Use a teaspoon to scrape the middle out of the cucumbers. Do this carefully, taking out just the soft part with the seeds. Put a double thick piece of absorbent kitchen paper on a plate and put the pieces of cucumber, cut sides down, on it to dry.

2 Put the soft cheese in a basin. Cut the ham or chicken into thin strips. Cut the strips across into very small dice. Add the ham to the cheese and mix well.

3 Put a little of the cheese into each piece of cucumber. Use a teaspoon and a knife to push it into the hole in the middle of the cucumber. Place the stuffed cucumber on a plate and put a sprig of parsley on top.

Strawberry tartlets

1 quantity pastry as for Mini Flans
2 tablespoons icing sugar
1 teaspoon vanilla essence
500 g/1 lb strawberries
100 g/4 oz strawberry jam
1 tablespoon water

Makes 15

Set the oven at 200°C/400°F/gas 6. Prepare all the ingredients for the pastry and make it following the recipe. Add the icing sugar to the dry mixture when you have rubbed the fat into the flour. Add the vanilla essence with the water. Line 15 patty tins following the recipe.

Prick the pastry cases 2 or 3 times with a fork. Bake them for 10–15 minutes, until they are lightly browned. Set out a heatproof mat. Use oven gloves to take the tins from the oven and then put it on the mat. Turn the heat off.

Leave the pastry cases in the tins for 5 minutes, then carefully lift them out using a palette knife. Put them on a wire rack to cool.

Wash and dry the strawberries. Twist the stalks and pull out the thin cores.

Put the jam in a basin with the water. Put some water into a small saucepan and put it on the hob. Put the basin on the saucepan and turn the heat to medium. Stir the jam until it has melted. Turn off the heat. Leave the basin over the hot water.

Fill the tartlet cases with strawberries. Cut some of the strawberries in half if they are very big. Use oven gloves to take the basin of jam off the water. Brush the melted jam all over the strawberries in the tartlets. Leave to set before serving.

▸ Open rolls ◂

4 finger rolls
50 g / 2 oz butter or margarine
4 cheese slices
24 slices cucumber

Makes 8

Split the rolls in half. Put the butter in a basin and soften it with a spoon. Spread the butter or margarine on the rolls.

Cut the cheese slices in half. Cut each half into 3 pieces. Put 3 pieces of cheese and 3 slices of cucumber on each roll, overlapping them alternately.

Arrange the rolls on a plate and cover with cling film until ready to serve.

▸ tuna fish dip ◂

200 g / 7 oz can tuna
100 g / 4 oz soft cheese with herbs and garlic
6 tablespoons mayonnaise or natural yogurt
salt and pepper

Serves 6

Open the can of tuna and drain off the liquid. Put the tuna in a basin and mash it with a form until it is all broken into small shreds.

Add the soft cheese and mix well. Stir in the mayonnaise with salt and pepper to taste.

Put the dip in a dish. Cover with cling film and put it in the refrigerator until you are ready to put the food on the table.

▸ pâté toasts ◂

100 g / 4 oz smooth pâté
12 Melba toasts
3–4 radishes
12 parsley sprigs

Makes 12

If the pâté is firm, put it in a basin and soften it by beating with a wooden spoon. Carefully spread the pâté on the Melba toasts. Do this flat on a board. The Melba toasts will break if you try to spread the pâté on them on a plate.

Cut the radishes into thin slices. Arrange some slices of radish and a sprig of parsley on each piece of toast. Put the Pâté Toasts on a plate and cover with cling film until ready to serve.

▸· Spicy Sausage bites ·◂

8 skinless sausages
1 teaspoon curry powder
1 clove garlic
1 tablespoon tomato ketchup
1 tablespoon natural yogurt or lemon juice
salt and pepper
1 tablespoon vegetable oil
1 small jar cocktail onions
1 grapefruit (optional)

Makes 32

1 Cut the sausages into 4 pieces. Put the curry powder in a large basin. Crush the garlic in a garlic crusher over the basin. Scrape all the bits from the outside of the crusher.

2 Add the tomato ketchup, yogurt or lemon juice to the curry powder. Sprinkle in a little salt and pepper. Put the pieces of sausage in the basin and mix well with a spoon. Carry on mixing up the sausages until all the pieces are flavoured with the curry paste.

3 Put a frying pan on the hob. Add the oil and turn the heat to medium. After 1 minute the oil will be hot and it will run freely over the pan if you tilt it. Add all the sausages. Cook for 15–20 minutes, stirring the sausages often so they brown all over.

4 Put a double thick piece of absorbent kitchen paper in a bowl. Turn the heat off. Tip all the sausages on to the paper. Shake the paper a little, then leave the sausages to cool.

5 Drain the onions. Thread each piece of sausage on to a cocktail stick with an onion. Put all the bites on a plate or stick them into a grapefruit.

▸· homemade lemonade ·◂

2 large lemons
175 g / 6 oz sugar
4 tablespoons water
1 large bottle sparkling mineral water
ice cubes
lemon slices, to serve (optional)

Makes 8 glasses

1 Grate the rind off both lemons on a fine grater. Put the rind in a saucepan. Cut the lemons in half and squeeze out all their juice. Add this to the pan.

2 Add the sugar and water to the pan. Put the pan on the hob and turn the heat to medium. Cook, stirring until the sugar has dissolved completely. Turn the heat off. Leave the lemon syrup to cool.

3 Put the cold syrup in a jug, topped up with mineral water. Add ice cubes and lemon slices if you like.

▶ easy cherry trifle ◀

1 large Swiss roll
3 tablespoons orange juice
425 g/15 oz can cherry pie filling
425 g/15 oz can custard
150 ml/¼ pint double cream
25 g/1 oz flaked almonds
6–8 maraschino or glacé cherries
6–8 small strips angelica

Serves 4–6

Cut the Swiss roll into thin slices. Put them in the bottom of a glass dish and about a third of the way up the side. Put any extra slices in a second layer on the bottom of the dish. Sprinkle the orange juice over the Swiss roll. Open the can of pie filling and use a spoon to spread it evenly over the Swiss roll.

Open the can of custard and pour it into a bowl, scraping all the custard out of the can. Put the cream in a basin and use a whisk to whip it until it stands in soft peaks. Add all the cream to the custard. Use a spatula to scrape the basin. Use a large metal spoon to fold the cream into the custard. Spread this all over the cherry pie filling.

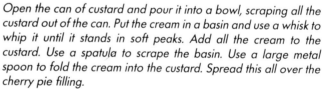
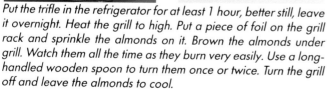

Put the trifle in the refrigerator for at least 1 hour, better still, leave it overnight. Heat the grill to high. Put a piece of foil on the grill rack and sprinkle the almonds on it. Brown the almonds under grill. Watch them all the time as they burn very easily. Use a long-handled wooden spoon to turn them once or twice. Turn the grill off and leave the almonds to cool.

Sprinkle the almonds over the trifle. Stick a small piece of angelica into each cherry. Arrange the cherries around the trifle just before serving it.

hazelnut truffles

simple coffee cake truffles

175g/6 oz chocolate
50 g/2 oz unsalted butter
50 g/2 oz toasted chopped skinned hazelnuts
1 tablespoon orange juice
1 tablespoon single cream or fromage frais
or Greek-style yogurt
cocoa powder for coating

Makes about 20

100g/4 oz chocolate
175 g/6 oz plain cake
2 teaspoons instant coffee
2 tablespoons boiling water
chocolate vermicelli for coating

Makes about 20

1 Break the chocolate into pieces and put them in a heatproof basin. Add the butter. Pour some water into a small saucepan and put it on the hob. Turn the heat to medium.

2 Stand the basin over the saucepan of water. Stir the chocolate and butter until both are completely melted. Do not allow the water to boil up at all. Turn the heat to low if the water begins to boil.

3 Turn the heat off and use oven gloves to lift the basin off the saucepan. Stir in the hazelnuts and orange juice. Leave the mixture to cool for about 30 minutes.

4 Stir the cream, fromage frais or yogurt into the chocolate, then put the basin in the refrigerator until the chocolate is firm enough to shape into balls. This will take about 45 minutes. It can be left for longer, then allowed to stand at room temperature for a while to soften slightly.

5 Put a small pile of cocoa on a plate. Set out about 20 paper sweet cases. Wash your hands under cold water and dry them. Try to keep your hands cold while you roll the truffles to stop you getting into a sticky mess!

6 Take a teaspoonful of the mixture and drop it on the cocoa. Roll it quickly into a ball and put it in a paper sweet case. Shape all the remaining truffles then put them in the refrigerator for at least 1 hour before packing them in a box. Cover with cling film. Add a bow and a tag.

Break the chocolate into squares and put them in a heatproof basin. Pour some water into a small saucepan and put it on the hob. Turn the heat to medium. Stand the basin over the saucepan. Stir the chocolate until it melts. Turn the heat to low if the water begins to boil.

Turn the heat off and use oven gloves to lift the basin off the saucepan.

Put the cake in a bowl. Wash and dry your hands. Crumble the cake with your fingertips until it is all in tiny crumbs.

Put the coffee in a cup and add the boiling water. Stir well. Use a teaspoon to sprinkle this coffee all over the cake. Pour the melted chocolate over the cake. Scrape all the chocolate out of the basin.

Use a spoon to mix the cake with the chocolate and coffee. Stir it for some time until it is all really well mixed up.

Put a small pile of chocolate vermicelli on a plate. Set out about 20 paper sweet cases on a baking tray. Wash and dry your hands again.

Take small spoonfuls of the mixture and shape it into balls. Roll the balls in the vermicelli, then put them into paper cases. Put the truffles in the refrigerator for at least 1 hour before you pack them in a box and cover with cling film. Add a bow and a tag.

▶·Sweet popcorn·◀

2 tablespoons vegetable oil
2 tablespoons popping corn
2 tablespoons sugar

Makes 1 bag

1 You will need a fairly large saucepan which has a lid. Have a heatproof basin ready to hold the cooked popcorn. Pour the oil into the pan and put it on the hob. Heat the oil over medium heat for about 2 minutes.

2 Add all the corn to the pan and put the lid on. Turn the heat to high until the corn begins to pop. When the corn is popping turn the heat to the lowest setting. Shake the pan occasionally and cook the corn until the popping has stopped.

POPCORN SPECIALS

★ *Popcorn is good savoury as well as sweet. Do not add the sugar. Instead, add a knob of butter and 2 tablespoons of grated Parmesan cheese to the corn and stir for about 1 minute. Sprinkle with a little salt and paprika, then leave to cool.*

★ *Instead of sugar, trickle 2 tablespoons honey over the popcorn and stir for a few seconds until the corn is golden. Turn into the basin to cool.*

★ *Mix the cold corn with raisins and nuts to make a bag of mixed nibbles.*

3 Use oven gloves to lift the lid off the pan. Sprinkle the sugar over the popcorn and stir well. Turn the heat to a high setting and stir the corn until the sugar melts and browns. This should take less than a minute. Take care not to overcook the popcorn or the sugar will burn.

4 When the corn is lightly browned and beginning to stick together, turn it all into the basin and leave it until it is cold. Do not taste the popcorn until it is cold as the caramelized sugar is very hot.

5 Pour cold water into the saucepan to soak otherwise the sugar hardens on it. Pack the cold popcorn in a polythene bag and seal it with a metal tie. Tie ribbon and a tag on the bag.

▸·toffee apples·◂

4 red apples
4 wooden skewers
225 g / 8 oz sugar
150 ml / ¼ pint water

Makes 4

Wash and thoroughly dry the apples, then polish them with absorbent kitchen paper until they shine. Place a piece of non-stick cooking paper on a baking tray. Stick a wooden skewer into the core of each apple and stand them on the baking tray.

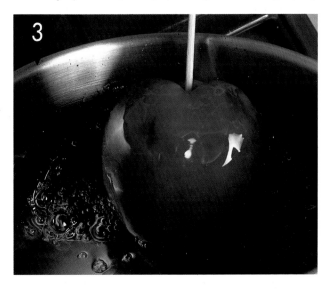

Put the sugar in a saucepan. Pour in the water. Put the pan on the hob. Turn the heat to medium and stir the sugar and water until the sugar has dissolved completely. Do not stir the syrup again. Turn the heat to high and bring the syrup to the boil. Turn the heat down slightly but keep the syrup boiling and bubbling rapidly.

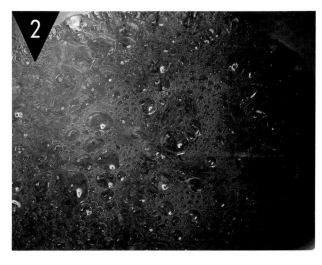

Watch the syrup all the time but do not stir it. After a while it will begin to change colour, turning very pale brown. Once it begins to turn brown it will brown quickly.

When it is slight golden colour (like syrup) turn the heat off. Hold the apples by their sticks and dip them quickly in the caramel. Tilt the pan slightly if necessary to coat the apples and twist them around.

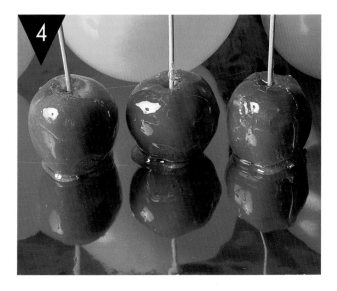

Let the excess caramel drip off back into the basin, then twist each apple to catch the last of the drips and put it back on the tray. Leave until the caramel is cold and hard. Do not keep the apples longer than 2 days or they become very sticky.